BLACKSMITHING FOR BEGINNERS

*20 Secrets Every Novice Should
Know Before Starting*

WES SANDER

TABLE OF CONTENTS

INTRODUCT ION

Iron is a metal that is found in abundance on Earth; in fact, it is the most abundant metal of all. It is not only found on Earth, but it is also abundant in the sun. It is an important part of steel, and plants need iron, just like humans, as it helps with oxygenation in our blood.

In its purest form, iron is a hard substance but a brittle one that is prone to corrosion when exposed to the various elements such as fire or moisture. Iron makes up approximately 90% of refined metals and is mixed with carbon to form an alloy we know as steel.

Steel is one of the most used metals in industries, such as construction, car manufacturing, civil engineering, and so on. Mixed with other metals like chromium it can create stainless steel, which is one of the most common metals used to make the cutlery we eat with.

In order to strengthen iron and make it more resistant to corrosion, it can be mixed with other metal compounds. For instance, when mixed with manganese, it becomes more durable. Nickel not only makes it durable but also more heat resistant, and to help it maintain its hardness tungsten, it is usually added to iron.

A Bit of Blacksmith History

Archeologists believe that iron has been used by humans for over 5,000 years, and some of the earliest iron used came from iron meteorites. The Journal of Archaeological Science published an article in 2013 about iron beads that were dated to be from around 3200 BC from ancient Egypt and found that these beads were made from iron meteorites.

The Iron Age followed the Bronze Age, a period in time where humans started to make various utensils, pots, tools, and weapons from iron. It is believed that the start of the Iron Age saw a cultural decline for great nations such as Ancient Greece. It was not that iron was not around before the Iron Age, but mostly because it was seen as an inferior metal, and bronze, a more durable metal, was the one chosen.

It is thought that the Hittites, who lived in Anatolia, or Turkey as we know it today, are thought to be the first to have forged steel. Once the steel was introduced to the world, it started to replace bronze as the metal of choice. But even before steel became the metal of choice ancient artisans perfected the art of shaping metal. Although we don't give it a moment's thought, we can on some level, thank these ancient blacksmiths for the great civilizations we have today.

Blacksmiths were the cornerstone of everything back then, they were relied upon to hand forge each knife, fork, pot, pan, weapon, wagon axles, and anything that needed shaped metal. Not only did they make tools, utensils, and such for others, but they had to create their own tools too. Some experts believe that the strength of an entire village or even city back then depended on how good their blacksmiths were.

But, as with everything, as time moved on, humans found ways to perfect and automate the art of creating things that were once forged by the hard-working hands of the local blacksmith. Where once the trade of a blacksmith was quite a thriving one, today it is part of the artisan trade that has faded into obscurity like the stonemasons. However, there are still those that are needed, just like a stonemason, because there are just some things that machines cannot replicate.

Before getting started, there are a few general things every aspiring blacksmith should know:

- **Where did the term "blacksmith" come from?**

  - A lot of people refer to blacksmiths as ironsmiths. This is true as they do mainly work with iron.
  - Although when referring to the artist as a blacksmith, the black part of the name is thought to come from the color iron turns when it is heated and exposed to air. This is a reaction caused by iron-oxide and is why iron is referred to as black metal.
  - There is a bit of debate about the meaning of the "smith" part of the word.

    - Some linguists believe that it comes from an old English word which is actually spelled "Smythe." Smythe means to strike.

- Others think that is may have come from a German word, "smithaz." Smithaz is used in reference to a skilled worker such as a gunsmith, locksmith, and shoesmith.

- **What is the Smithy?**

  - A smithy is a skilled worker workshop, where they keep their tools and it is where they work from — it is where they forge metal into objects.

FREE BONUSES FOR THE READERS

First of all, I want to congratulate you on taking the right steps to learn and improve your blacksmithing skills, by buying this book.

Few people take action on improving their craft, and you are one of them.

To get the most out of this book, I have 3 resources for you that will help you jumpstart you with knifemaking as well.

Since you are now a reader of my books, I want to extend a hand, and improve our author-reader relationship, by offering you all 3 of these bonuses for FREE.

All you have to do is visit **https://www.elitebladesmith-ingmasterclass.com/free-bonus** and enter the e-mail where you want to receive these resources.

These bonuses will help you:

1. Make more money when selling your knives to customers
2. Save time while knife making

Here's what you receive for FREE:

1. Bladesmith's Guide to Selling Knives
2. Hunting Knife Template
3. Stock Removal Cheat Sheet

Here is a brief description of what you will receive in your inbox:

1. Bladesmith's Guide to Selling Knives

Do you want to sell your knives to support your hobby, but don't know where to start?

Are you afraid to charge more for your knives?

Do you constantly get low-balled on the price of your knives?

'Bladesmith's Guide to Selling Knives' contains simple but fundamental secrets to selling your knives for profit.

Both audio and PDF versions are included.

Inside this book you will discover:

- How to **make more money** when selling knives and swords to customers (Higher prices)
- The **<u>hidden-in-plain-sight</u>** location that is perfect for selling knives (Gun shows)
- Your **biggest 'asset'** that you can leverage to charge higher prices for your knives, and **make an extra $50 or more** off of selling the same knife.
- 4 critical mistakes you could be making, that are **holding you back from selling your knife for what it's truly worth**
- The ideal number of knives you should bring to a knife show
- 5 online platforms where you can sell your knives
- 9 key details you need to mention when selling your knives online, that will increase the customers you get

2. Hunting Knife Template for Stock Removal

Tired of drawing plans when making a knife?

Not good at CAD or any sort of design software?

Make planning and drawing layouts a 5-second affair, by downloading this classic bowie knife design that you can print and grind on your preferred size of stock steel.

Here's what you get:

- Classic bowie knife design **you can print and paste** on stock steel and start grinding
- Remove the hassle of planning and drawing the knife layout during knife making
- Detailed plans included, <u>to ensure straight and clean grind lines</u>

3. Stock Removal Cheat Sheet

Do you need to quickly lookup the correct knife making steps, while working on a knife in your workshop?

Here's what you get:

- Make your knife through stock removal in just **14 steps**
- <u>Full stock removal process</u>, done with 1084 steel
- **Quick reference guide** you can print and place in your workshop

As mentioned above, to get access to this content, go to <u>*https://www.elitebladesmithingmasterclass.com/free-bonus*</u> and enter the e-mail where you want to receive these 3 resources.

DISCLAIMER: By signing up for the free content you are also agreeing to be added to my bladesmithing e-mail list, to which I send helpful bladesmithing tips and promotional offers.

I would suggest you download these resources before you proceed further, because knives make great blacksmithing projects.

CHAPTER 1: 20 TIPS FOR THE ASPIRING BLACKSMITH TO KNOW

Here are some tips to help you improve your skills and knowledge with metal and various tools.

1. How to Swing Your Hammer

Swinging a hammer seems easy, pick up the hammer and whack. That may be okay for someone that is using a hammer every now and then to fix something, but when you are doing it continuously, you are going to find there is a right way and wrong way to swing a hammer.

- **The weight of the hammer** — choose the weight of the hammer according to the task you need it to do. A lighter hammer is not always the best choice as you may need to apply more force to get the job done. This is just going to end up hurting you. A hammer that is too heavy may damage the metal and you.
- **Gripping the hammer** — have a comfortable grip on the hammer. You do not need to have a death grip on it, just enough to make sure it is going to stay in your hand when you swing. It must be comfortably fitted in your hand.

- **The lift**

  - Power hit — use the rebound of the anvil to help lift your hammer hit after hit.
  - Use your wrist — use your wrist to put a snap into the hit.
  - Use your elbow — use your elbow to bring the hammer up to your body before lifting it.
  - Use the shoulder — use your shoulder to lift from the body up to over your shoulder.

- **The hit**

  - Drop the hammer from the shoulder.
  - Through the elbow.
  - Snap the wrist as you hit the metal and the repeat from the lift.

- **What not to do**

  - Small pounding hits from the elbow only using short hard bursts.
  - Put your thumb on top of your hammer handle.
  - Long pounding bursts that move your entire body up and down as you hit.
  - Use short little bursts with your hammer elbow tucked against your body and hitting from your elbow.

- **Use the hammer handle to increase power**

  - For harder hits, hold the hammer more to the back of the handle.

- Holding the middle of the hammer gives a bit more control.
- Holding the handle against the head of the hammer is for more delicate or tightly controlled hits.

2. The Different Types of Strikes

When you are forging metal, it does not mean that you are just knocking the metal into shape. You are using a skill to forge the metal. In so doing, you are not only using the hammer but the anvil as well. When you are working with metal forging you are using two tools to shape the metal as it gets shaped between the pounding of the hammer and the anvil.

There are different types of strikes.

- **Parallel strike**

This is when you hit down on the heated metal with the hammer strikes being parallel to anvil beneath the heated metal. It is usually done with the cross preen hammer as it tends to hit the angle for this strike just right.

- **Angle strike**

This is when you hold the piece of heated metal at an angle to the anvil and when you strike the heated metal with the hammer, the hammer is at an angle to the anvil. This also tends to form an angle in the metal, typically used when you are trying to forge the tip or part of the tip of the metal to a point. This strike can be done with any type of hammer using either of the faces of the hammer.

- **Half-face near strike**

The half-face near strike is when the heated metal is struck with the hammer just below the metals tips to form an indented square step in the bottom part of the metal. It does this because the heated metal is struck where it hangs off the anvil. It is called a half-face hit because the face of the hammer is aligned halfway on the anvil and half off of the anvil as it strikes the metal to form the step indent.

It is called a near strike because the heated metal is struck on the near side of the anvil (the side the blacksmith is standing on).

- **Half-face far strike**

The half-face far strike is when the heated metal is hit somewhere near the front end or middle of the heated metal. The heated metal lies across the anvil and is struck by the hammer where it crosses the far edge of the anvil. This is done to make the same type of step in the metal as for the near-face strike. Only it is done on the far side of the anvil.

The hammer hits the metal with its face aligned halfway on the anvil and half off of the far side of the anvil on the far side.

- **Edge hammer near strike**

The nearside-edge hammer blow is when the hammer strikes the heated metal with the head of the hammer aligned with the near edge of the anvil. If you were to perform this strike without the metal, you would be hitting the anvil with the head of the hammer right near the near edge of the anvil. The face of the hammer would never go off the anvil edge but very close to it. It is usually delivered as an angled blow.

This strike is normally used to create a flat or round tip at the front of the heated metal.

- **Edge hammer far strike**

The far-side-edge hammer blow is when the hammer strikes the heated metal with the head of the hammer aligned with the far edge of the anvil. If you were to perform this strike without the metal, you would be hitting the anvil with the head of the hammer right near the far edge of the anvil. The face of the hammer would never go off the anvil. This strike is hit at an angle to the anvil.

Usually, this is used to create an indent or a thin neck type shape in the heated metal.

- **Back face strike**

  This is usually done with the back part of the hammer and is normally used to upset the metal (make it shorter and thicker). This can be done by holding the metal flat on the anvil and hitting the top of the meatal backward over the far end of the anvil or clamping the heated metal in a vice or vice Hardie hole attachment and then hitting directly on the heated edge of the metal with the thicker back end of the hammer until you have the desired size, thickness, or shape.

- **Shearing face strike**

  This is a strike where you would hold the heated metal over the anvil and hit it with the hammer face hitting the metal until it completely breaks the necessary part off.

3. The Three Essential Blacksmith Tools

There are three tools of the trade you are going to need before you can start to forge steel. If you are serious about wanting to become a blacksmith as a career or a hobbyist, then you are going to need to have your own smithy or spruce up your workshop with a few basic items that are needed to bend and control metal to your will.

- **A Heat Source**

  The heat source is better known as the **forge** is one of the most important things that a blacksmith needs as it is where the metal gets heated.

- **Something to pound the metal with**

  This would be a **hammer** that is used to pound the heated metal to manipulate it into shape.

- **Something to pound the metal on**

  The is the **anvil**, which is usually a steel block

  A lot of potential blacksmiths are put off by thinking that it is going to cost a fortune in equipment to get started. But a seasoned blacksmith will tell you that you do not need the top of the line equipment to do great steelwork.

  When you are starting out in any new trade it is best to start slow and learn to make your own tools. This allows you to learn and grow before splashing out on expensive stuff.

The Forge

There are many types and styles of forges, the range from the top of the line gas or coal forge to a simple wood fire.

A good forge is based on how well it keeps the fire contained within it, it needs to be able to heat up the metal so it can be pounded into shape.

The forge should be made out of either:

- **Brick** — brick is made under extreme heat and as such has the ability to expand and contract under extreme heat conditions. That is why most chimneys are made from brick, it also traps the heat within.
- **Cast Iron** — can withstand extreme heat and is why most old fashioned wood ovens were made from cast iron. Cast iron also traps the heat in.

Both brick and iron will be able to create a solid forge that is sturdy and can properly contain the fire for the forge.

Four Main Parts of the Forge

1. **The bellows** — this is the blower that controls (stokes) the fire.
2. **The fire pot** — this is where the fire will be and over which the metal gets heated by the blacksmith.
3. **The tuyere** — this is a grate that sits beneath the fire pot and looks like a large sink drain. The tuyere usually has a pipe attached to the drain that ends by the bellows. This is how the bellow forces the air up to the fire pot to feed the fire.
4. **Chimney** — the chimney is an important part of the forge if it is in an enclosed area as it the forge needs a way for the smoke to escape.

The chimney for a forge acts the same as it would for a fireplace or woodstove. Forges that are open-air do not need a chimney as the smoke is released into the air.

Two types of Forge Fuels

Forges have two types of fuels sources and these are:

1. Solid fuel

- **Coal** — is the most popular solid fuel used for forges and can burn at temperatures of up to 2,000° Fahrenheit.
- **Coke** — is a pure carbon fuel and can burn temperatures of up to 2,000° Fahrenheit.

2. Gas fuel

- **Propane** — is the more popular and more portable of the gas used for forges. Gas fuels tend to burn a lot cleaner than the solid fuels do, but they do not get to the temperatures that the solid fuel does.

The Hammer(s)

The hammer is another important tool that every blacksmith is going to need. To start with, you will only need one good hammer that can be used for most work. As you become more involved in the craft you will find that you slowly build up a collection of different hammers that you will use on various projects.

Characteristics of a Good Hammer

- It should be light enough so that you work steadily.
- It should weigh around about 1-½ lbs. to 3 lbs. at most.
- Make sure it has a good solid grip that will not break easily and is non-slip.

The Anvil

The anvil is another essential tool that a black-smith uses to pound and mold the hot metal on.

There are many different styles of anvils, they can range from $100 up to thousands of dollars. But, when you start off, you do not need anything fancy. In fact, a lot of starter blacksmiths used to cut off pieces of railway track, which makes for an excellent anvil as it is usually made from good solid steel.

You can even use a solid piece of metal, as long as you can secure, and it will withstand both the heat of the metal along with the pounding of the metal. But you can still find a good-quality cheaper anvil or even scan your local papers or secondhand websites for owners selling theirs off to find some great deals.

Two Most Popular Metal Types for Anvils

A good anvil will last for years and some of the most sought after anvils today are the ones that are 80 years and older. They tend to be worn in and built to last.

Anvils are usually made from either:

- **Cast iron** — you can tell the difference when you hit a metal hammerhead against the anvil. The cast iron anvil will have a dull thud as the cast iron absorbs the hammering.
- **Steel** — the steel anvil will have a ring to it as it pushes the hammering outwards and into the metal being hammered. Kind of like the difference between the dull noise a plain glass makes as opposed to the ring of a pure crystal glass.

Two Most Popular Anvil Styles

You will find many different shapes, sizes, and styles of anvils on the market. Which one you choose is a choice you make depending on what suits your needs.

Two Most Common Styles

- **European Style** — this anvil has two horns, one on either end of the anvil. The one horn will be completely round and there will be no step up to the table of the anvil from the round horn. The Hardie hole (square hole) is found at the end of the table just above the round horn.

The other side of the anvil has a boat-shaped horn that is triangular and the pritchel hole (the round hold) is usually located above this horn at the end of the table. Smaller European anvils sometimes do not have a pritchel hole on. These anvils also tend to have a thicker waist than the London style ones, which makes it a lot sturdier.

- **London Style** — this anvil was made popular around the 1800s. It can be defined by its narrow waist, long slightly sloped horn, chiseled cutting block (this is the table or step), and a steep heel. It has quite a large face and comes with both a Hardie hole (the square hole) and a pritchel hole (the small round hole) these holes can be found near the heel of the anvil.
- **Setting up the anvil** — the anvil should either have a stand of its own that is bolted to the floor so it is stable. Or it could be bolted to a workbench. The main thing about the anvil is to get it to the perfect height for you to work on.
- To get the anvil at the perfect height for you, you should be able to stand next to it, make a fist with your hands and your knuckles should be able to rest comfortably on the anvil body with your arms hanging straight down your side.

The Hardie Hole and the Pritchel Hole

Most anvils will come with two holes on top of them. These holes are the:

- **Hardie hole** — this hole is the square hole and it is used to stabilize various attachments that fit into the anvil to help the blacksmith shape or grip the metal he is working with. Various shapes can be fit into the Hardie hole to help the blacksmith to manipulate the metal. The great thing about this is, as a blacksmith, you can create your own attachments to fit the Hardie hole and help to create unique pieces.

- **Pritchel hole** — this hole is used to enable the blacksmith to punch holes in the metal piece he is working on. Without this hole, if the blacksmith needs to make holes in the metal he is working on, it will hit the anvil. Punching a hole in the metal over the pritchel hole will allow that punch to go right through the hot metal.

4. How to Test the Carbon Content in Steel

Carbon is what is added to iron to make it more durable and what makes steel. There are two types of typical steel alloy:

- Carbon steel — this is a combination of iron and carbon.

- Stainless steel — this is a combination of iron and chromium.

The amount of carbon that gets added to iron is what determines the steel's use.

- **Wrought iron** — this is iron that has the lowest content of carbon in it. Wrought iron is used in applications such as fencing.
- **Mild steel** — this is iron that has a medium amount of carbon in and is used in applications that need a bit more strength and durability to the alloy, such as structural use for buildings or bridges.
- **High-carbon steel** — this is iron that has a lot of carbon in it, as its name implies. This type of steel is used for things like steel wire or springs.
- **Cast iron** — this is iron that has ultra-high carbon content. It is usually very heavy. Some pots and cauldrons are made from cast iron.

Steel does not always come labeled with the carbon content in it, but there is a simple way to test the carbon content in the metal.

What you will need:

- Grinder
- Normal grinding wheel
- Metal to test the carbon content

How to test the metal:

- Turn on the grinder.
- Take the metal, and holding it safely, apply parts of it to the moving grinding wheel.
- Observe the sparks and the way they flow from the metal when it is being ground.

What to look for:

By observing the spark patterns of the steel being ground, it will give you a good indication of what the content of carbon in the steel is. Steel, as previously discussed falls into basic categories of low, medium, and high.

- **Low carbon steel** — produces sparks in long fine tails with no forks or short spritzers of sparks.
- **Medium carbon steel** — produces sparks in more forks and sprays. Instead of a long fine tail of sparks, they will seem like smaller broken pieces of the tail and have a wider spark area.
- **High carbon steel** — the sparks look like short bursts of spray and it has many little forks in it. It looks more like a sparkler you would put on a birthday cake.

5. **Ideas for a Basic Layout for Your Smithy's Work Area**

The layout of the smithy is a personal thing, but there are a few tips one could use to make it more efficient and streamlined as well as some points on what not to put in certain places.

The most important thing is to ensure you have enough space for your smithy and stay within your budgetary limits. It is good to want a huge shop, but really, it is best to start off with what you can afford just makes sure you have room to grow should you need to.

Remember these tips are only suggestions!

- **The ceiling** — this should be as high as you can make it, especially if you have a gas forge. Around 10 feet is usually a great height for the ceiling as the heat will not accumulate near to where you are, hot air rises and the higher the ceiling the more heat will be let out of the work area.
- **The chimney** — if you have a solid-fuel forge, you will need a chimney. The higher the chimney, the more efficient it is because it gets a stronger differential pressure and hence a better draft.
- **Door(s)** — when people are planning their workspace, one of two main things they tend to overlook are the two most obvious things. The first being the door, until you try to move equipment into the workshop. The best kind of door to have in any workshop is a double door. One that can half shut while using the

other as a normal door. This will make sure that most standard equipment can be moved in and out of the smithy with no problems.

Double doors are also great for opening up more air into the room should the need arise for better ventilation.

- **Window(s)** — these are also usually over-looked in a plan for a workshop and are vital for both ventilation and natural light. Ensure that they can open to at least three phases.
- **Floor** — another personal choice but the best floors for a workshop are always cement ones. They are easier to clean up and do not get damaged as quickly as the wooden one. If any embers hit them they are less likely to burn.
- You can push heavy objects around on it with no problem, you can use various mats or ply-wood to soften the area where you stand. They are a lot more level than dirt floors, you can anchor things to them if you need to and you do not get a whole lot of kicked up dirt as you do with dirt floors. Plus, on dirt floors, it is difficult to find small things you drop, and they have all the dirt on them when you do.
- **Powering the smithy** — you are going to need electricity in the smithy so look to posi-tion the power plugs in crucial places along the walls.

- Look at about 230 volts with around 60 to 100 amps. If you are using any type of industrial equipment you may need to look at a 3-phase with around 500 volts.

- **Lighting**

  You are going to want a well-lit smithy and not a dark one. Go for fluorescent lighting as it lasts the longest and you get some powerful lights that will give you a well-lit area that will not strain your eyes.

- **Layout** — as stated before, the layout of the smithy is a personal thing. It is how the blacksmith finds his workflow.

  - **A solid-fuel forge** should have the chimney side to a wall, but the actual pot should be open and have room for the blacksmith to work from both sides. A rule of thumb is, you should be able to lay an 8-foot metal bar neatly over the pot and be able to comfortably be able to access it from the left or right side of the forge.

  - **A gas forge** can be positioned where it is convenient and there is enough air. Always make sure that the gas forge is sturdy and very stable with no chance of tippling or collapsing.

  - It is not advisable to put the forge in a room corner with it is awkward to get to or you cannot access both sides of the forge.

- Usually, a smithy is laid in a triangular type shape with the **anvil** as the center-piece.

- One side of the triangle will have the forge, the other a nice workbench, and the other you can have your vice and tool cabinet(s).

- Do not put tools such as grinders, sand-ers, welders, gas tanks, etc., near the forge. You keep these on a workbench that does not interfere with your anvil as well.

- It is good practice to keep all your tools clean and packed away once you have finished using them. This includes the anvil as tools that are looked after will last a lot longer.

- The forge should be clean out, and the chimney and blower checked each time it is done being used. This ensures that you can get right to work the next time you need to use it.

6. Fundamental Techniques of Blacksmithing

- **Drawing out metal**

This is the technique that a blacksmith uses to make a piece of heated metal longer. The metal will get thinner as it lengthens, which will also decrease the cross-section of the metal.

- **Tapering**

  This is the technique that a blacksmith uses to bring a piece of heated metal to a point. It looks a lot like a sharpened pencil or a tent stake. The metal will get a bit thinner at the point as it becomes tapered.

- **Bending**

This is the technique that a blacksmith uses to bend a piece of heated metal into a shape like a horseshoe, curtain rings, and so forth. The blacksmith bends the metal in several different ways. He could use a shaped attachment placed in the Hardie hole to bend the metal around. He could use the anvil horn to bend and shape the metal on, or even the corners of the anvil's table.

- **Upsetting**

This is the technique that a blacksmith uses to make a piece of heated metal thicker. The metal piece is held upright as the blacksmith pounds the metal back onto itself. The metal will become shorter, and it will increase the cross-section of the metal. This is usually done when a thicker piece of metal is needed for things like ground pegs and table legs.

- **Spreading**

  This is the technique that a blacksmith uses to widen or spread a piece of heated metal. The metal will get thinner or flatter as it widens and spreads out. This is done to make things like spoons, or a fishtail for ornamental reasons, and is how blacksmiths in ancient times make various weapons like swords.

- **Punching**

  This is the technique that a blacksmith uses to punch a hole in a piece of heated metal. The blacksmith will make the hole by securing the metal to be punched, and then using a punch (a special type of hammer with a long snout), he will knock a hole through a piece of metal. This is done for many reasons but usually in order to join two pieces of metal together or to attach the metal onto something.

- **Slitting**

  This is the technique that a blacksmith uses to make a slit at the end of a piece of heated metal. It can be used when the end of the metal needs to be bent or forked in different directions.

  When slitting, a blacksmith may need to work on one half of the slit at a time. If the slit between the two halves is not wide enough, the blacksmith may create a **convenience bend**. This is a bend he manipulates on the half of the slit that is not being worked on. It usually bends the one half away from the other, leaving just enough space to work on the other half. It is done in such a way as not to compromise the structure of the other half or break it.

- **Twisting**

This is the technique that a blacksmith uses to make a twist or twists in a piece of heated metal for convenience or ornamental appeal. The blacksmith will place the heated metal in a vice and secure, so he can use a wrench to place twists in the metal.

Twisting is quite an art to perfect especially when trying to twist a long piece of metal. The black-smith will twist a longer piece or complex twist piece in portions, which usually require the metal to be reheated and cooled several times.

He will cool the portion of the twist he is happy with so that it will not long twist, then reheat the portion he needs to continue twisting. It takes time and patience to master this technique.

7. Types of Hammers

One of the three essential blacksmiths tools is a hammer. While you will only need one to start off with, there are many different types and styles of hammers that are used by blacksmiths. Each one has its unique style and use. If you continue with blacksmithing, you may very well find you will eventually end up with a whole lot of different hammers.

- **Rounding Hammer**

The rounding hammer shapes heated metal evenly in all directions when the metal is pounded with the round face.

A rounding hammer usually has two faces to it, one face will be rounded while the other will be flat.

The flat face is used for smoothing out the metal, which is called planishing. This is where the metal is fine-tuned by being smoothed out and hammered into the desired shape.

The round face is used to pound the heated metal into shape in an even matter or to create an interior bend in the metal to create a nice rounded and better-finished bend.

This is the better hammer to use when you first start to shape a new piece of iron to get it evenly shaped out.

- **Cross Peen Hammer**

This hammer also has two faces or edges to it. The one edge has a flat face and the other end extends out to laterally from the head of the hammer to form a flat type of a point.

It is the pointed side of the cross peen that is most used. It is used to pound heated metal to get it to move perpendicularly from the peen. In other words, when the metal is pounded with the cross peen hammer, the hammer hits it in a left to right pounding motion this makes the metal move up and down. It is what is used mostly to lengthen or thin out metal, to flatten metal, etc.

- **Straight Peen Hammer**

  This hammer looks and is styled the same as the cross peen. But where the peen on the cross peen is horizontal, the straight peen hammer has a vertical peen.

  Where the cross peen hits the metal from a side to side manner to get it to move up and down, the straight peen hits the metal from top to bottom. This strike on a heated piece of metal makes it move out equally to either side, which is great for flattening the metal.

- **Diagonal Peen Hammer**

  This hammer looks a lot like the straight peen hammer with a more defined and chiseled flat end. The peen looks like it has been twisted to the side. This peen is used when a blacksmith needs to strike the iron at a diagonal to flatten out or straighten the metal, for instance, on a piece of metal where there are twists that need to be flattened or at an angle where the other two peen hammers are not capable.

- **Ball Peen Hammer**

This hammer will have a round ball head on the one of it called the ball peen. It is used when the blacksmith needs the heated metal to move out-wards and equally from where it is struck with the ball. If you are wanting to make a leaf pattern or something round like the head of a spoon, this is the best hammer to use.

8. Tongs

Tongs are not that necessary but are handy to have especially for shorter pieces of metal. A tong is used to clamp down on the metal being pounded to keep it steady for a more precise hit when pounding the metal into shape. Just like the different hammers, there are many different types of tongs with each one being unique in style and what it is used for. The thing they all have in common is the long handle.

- **Flat Jaw Tongs**

The flat jaw tongs are used to hold flat pieces of metal in place while the blacksmith hammers them into place and are very basic tongs.

- **V-Bit Tongs**

These tongs have V-shapes inside their jaws which is for clamping down on shapes that are thick and square or round. At the end of these tongs jaws is a round open part. This is handy for the clamping of metal objects that have a large head like that of a bolt.

- **Box Jaw Tongs**

As these tongs' name implies, they are shaped like a box. The top half of the jaw moves like a box lid while the bottom half of the tongs are shaped like the bottom half of a box.

These tongs come in different sizes in order to accommodate different sizes of metal as the heated metal has to fit perfectly in the box for the tongs to be able to grip it.

Blacksmiths usually have a few of these tongs in different sizes as it is a very safe tong to use. It holds the metal securely while the blacksmith works on it.

- **Scroll Tongs**

A scroll tong has two round jaws that help a blacksmith make lovely round bends or scrolls in heated in metal.

- **Wolf Jaw Tongs**

These tongs have two long jaws shaped much like a wolf's snout. They are the most versatile of the tongs and the most commonly used by black-smiths. The inside of the jaws is much like that of pliers as it has ridges that hold a better grip heated metal, so the blacksmith can work on it from all sides.

9. Chisels

There are many shapes and sizes of chisels depending on the work. They are used to help the blacksmith do things like creating a slit in the metal. The chisel is held on the place of the metal where the blacksmith wants to create the slit, and then he uses a hammer on the back of the chisel to knock the slit through.

As you build your tool collection, you will find you collect more and more chisels to meet your metal forging requirements.

10. Hold Down tools

Hold down tools are tools that help to hold down metal objects while the blacksmith works. There are a few ways they can do this, but the two most popular ways are:

- **Pritchel Hold Down**

This tool looks like a hook that usually has a tapered flat foot at the end of it. It is made out of spring steel with a slight give in it to allow it to slightly bend under pressure.

The tools long end gets placed in the pritchel hole, and the foot will hold down the metal placed beneath it on the anvil bench.

These can be bought or made by the blacksmith himself to his exact specifications.

- **Chain Hold Down**

This is a long strong chain that is weighted on one end and anchored on the other. The chain is placed over the heated metal with the weighted end hanging down on the opposite side of the anvil to where the blacksmith works. The anchor side will be securely wrapped around a solid object, like the table or bench leg the anvil is standing on, with a secure loop in the floor, especially for the anchor.

The chain holds the heated piece of metal in place, so the blacksmith can work with it.

11. Fuller

The fuller is used to shape iron into a U-shape. They can be handheld fullers or those that are stabilized in the Hardie hold. Some of them come with two handy sides, one side will have the typical wheel shape while the other will have two long thin long round jaws.

The heated metal is placed between these two jaws, and the blacksmith will hit the top jaw. The impact creates a U-shaped dent in the sides of the metal that was placed against the jaws.

12. Punch

A punch is used to punch a hole in the heated metal when hit with a hammer. Punches bear a very close resemblance to a hammer but will have a very long pointy snout at the one end and a flatter face on the back end where the hammer hits it.

They do come in different sizes. A punch needs to be cooled in cold water after each second or third strike into the heated metal. This is to stop it from getting too hot and dulling the point.

13. Blacksmith Vice

There are a few kinds of vices that a person can get, but the one that is commonly used by black-smiths is a leg vice or it can also be called a blacksmith's vice. It is a vice that is bolted to the end of a bench with a long leg that extends to the floor. This makes the vice able to withstand the heavy pounding that it will have to take when shaping metal.

Most normal type vices will not be able to take the force of the blows and that is one of the reasons a leg vice is also called a blacksmith vice.

14. Rasp

When metal is cut, it leaves a grainy edge that can be quite rough. This edge must be smoothed down. This is done by a rasp and is a tool that is commonly used by a farrier to file and smooth horseshoes.

A rasp looks like a large file made from steel with a lot of rough edges that are rubbed across the metal to smooth it.

15. Cone Mandrel

This tool looks like a long metal ice-cream cone. It has a wide round base that leads up to a more pointed and rounded top part.

It is used to make perfectly round metal shapes as the heated metal is placed on the top of it, pushed down to the part of the cone that meets the size requirement, then knocked into a rounded shape.

16. Personal Safety Items

- Masks

Some blacksmiths wear a mask or goggles to protect their face and eyes from stray metal castings, fire, etc. It is best to usually at least cover your mouth and nose when working in an environment where there is metal being worked or fire. Ideally, a blacksmith should wear protective eye gear. There are lots of embers and sparks that fly around when forging or working near the fire.

- Safety Aprons

A heavy-duty blacksmith apron is there to protect you from embers that may spit off in the fire and to stop getting accidentally singed by the metal. They also protect your clothes from the embers that fly off the heated metal or the fire. Modern-day leather aprons offer high protection without being heavy and bulky. Leather also protects the body from burns, if the embers can burn through clothes, that means they can and usually do touch the skin too.

- Safety Gloves

A strong pair of leather blacksmith gloves will protect your hands against the heat, cuts, and so on. Just like aprons protect your body and clothes from burns, a good pair of leather smithy gloves protect your hands. They also help to give a person a better grip on the metal as sometimes you need to hold the metals and not clamp it.

17. Different Types of Metal

There are many types of metal one can use for forging each has its benefits.

- **Alloy steel**

This is one of the most commonly used steels in the art of blacksmithing. This steel is usually a lot tougher and more durable than most other steel it consists of:

- Boron
- Chromium
- Iron
- Manganese
- Molybdenum
- Nickel
- Vanadium

- **Carbon steel**

Carbon steel is another popular steel used for forging. It is a tough metal that is not too difficult to work with. There are many different grades of carbon steel, mainly light, medium, and heavy. Each one with its own unique purpose, for instance, medium is good for gates.

Carbon steel is usually made up of:

- Carbon
- Iron
- Manganese
- Phosphorus
- Silicone

- **Stainless steel**

Stainless steel is popular for forging things that won't tarnish and have some durability. One of the most common pieces forged with this metal is cutlery, pots, and pans.

Stainless steel consists of:

- Carbon
- Chromium
- Iron

- **Wrought iron**

Wrought iron is a very tough and durable metal that is rather easy to work with as it is very malleable. It has a very low carbon content (usually less than 0.08%), it is also a semi-fused iron with slag inclusions that can be fibrous. When it is bent or etched, it gets a grain on it much like wood. That is why pots or grates, etc., made out of wrought iron more often than not have a roguish texture to them.

Wrought iron consists of:

- Carbon
- Iron
- Manganese
- Phosphorus
- Silicon
- Sulfur

18. Fire Control

Fire maintenance is a word you are going to come across in blacksmithing and it is the way the fire is controlled. A forge needs to allow the blacksmith to control the fire in the forge by increasing the flame to a large one or to decrease the flame to a smaller one that allows for a slow burn.

The fire gets controlled by what is called the bellows. Historically a bellows was a handheld pump that was used to stoke the fire with. These days, it needs a blower of some sort; some forges have a blower that is built into them.

The bellow needs to be able to blow air into the fire as and when the blacksmith requires the flame to quickly be increased or to slow it down to decrease the fire.

19. Fire Safety

No matter what type of forge you have, it means working with fire. There are always risks when working with fire, and as such, you should always implement safety precautions when working with the forge.

- The forge should always be sturdy. Make sure there is no risk of accidentally falling over.
- Make sure the forge is not close to anything flammable. If the forge is operational, think before you put any flammable material near it.
- Always have an emergency water source close to the forge for the sole purpose of fire control.
- Make sure there is some sort of a chimney that is kept clean and clear.
- There needs to be enough air coming into the fire as well as a free flow for the smoke to escape.
- Make sure there are set fire controls in place.

20. Making a Fire

You are going to want to be able to make the perfect fire in your coal forge. As discussed previously in this chapter under the three essential tools for a blacksmith, coal, and coke were discussed as the best solid fuel types for a forge fire.

Ideally, a forge fire must burn fast and very hot.

- To get the fire going you should take three to four pieces of newspaper and fold them into a donut shape and push a hole through the middle of it just like the hole in a donut.
- Place the newspaper donut at the very bottom of the clean forge over the vent where the blower blows air into the forge pot. Make sure the donut hold is lined up with the vent hole to let the air flow through.
- Light the newspaper to start the fire.
- Start to put a more solid form of fuel on top of the newspaper into the fire. This solid fuel type can be coal, which burns nice hot but contains a lot of carbon.
- Coke is the rock that is left behind after green coal has been burned. It tends to be high in carbon but low in sulfur. Using the coke left behind from a previous coal fire is the ideal coke to use for a forge fire.
- Once your fire starts to burn you will want to add coal as and when needed to sustain the fire for as long as you need it to burn.
- A gas forge only needs a person to turn on and light the gas to get the forge going.

CHAPTER 2: PROJECT 1 – MAKING A MARSHMALLOW ROD

This is a really simple project for a beginner to try their hand at. Plus, you do not need a lot of fancy equipment to get it up and running. This is a marshmallow roasting road that will teach you how to get a nice tapered edge and do some simple metal twists.

What you will need:

- **A heat source** — this could a forge or it could be something like the torch plumbers use to heat pipes with or a blow/cutting torch. It needs to be able to heat the metal.
- **An anvil** — if you do not have an anvil, you can use a piece of steel that is similar in composition and style to a railway track, as long as it is hard enough to take a beating and sturdy enough to support the beating. It must be sturdy and well stabilized as not to move when it is being pounded on. It should also have a semi-rounded nose or horn. This is needed to make the handle of the marshmallow sticks.
- **Water** — this can be a can of sorts. Do not use plastic it needs to be something that can withstand heat; even though the water is cold, you are going to be putting hot metal into it.

- **Hammer** — choose a hammer that is not too heavy, around 1.5 to 2.5 lbs. A rounding hammer would be perfect for this project.
- **Tongs** — something to grip the metal with if you do not have something like a box tong, V-shaped, or flat-faced tongs to hold and grip the metal with while you twist it. For this, you can try a pair of pliers.
- **Vice grip** — this is to hold the metal steady to put some simple twists in it.
- **Metal** — ¼-inch metal rods of your metal of choice and as many as you want to try and make.
- **Hard brush** — this is to clean off the metal once you have finished hammering it and it has cooled down to get rid of any carbon residue.

Method

1. Ready your forge or heat source.
2. Have all your tools handy.
3. Heat the top of the metal rod until the metal is glowing hot.
4. Place it with the tip on the table of the anvil.
5. Use the round face of the hammer to pound the tip of the metal into a point.
6. To do this, you hit and then turn the metal to the next side, pounding again and again as you turn the metal from side to side.
7. As it starts to thin and taper to a point, slow down a bit to taper it nicely.
8. You will know when it is done at the end.

9. Make sure the tip is cool and set by dipping it into the cold water.

10. Next, you are going to do a nice closed, curved handle to hold the marshmallow stick with and it is also handy if you want to hang them up for storing them.

11. To do this, heat the end that is not tapered until it is glowing hot.

12. Place the tip flat on the anvil, use the round face of the hammer to pound the tip into a small flat fishtail.

13. If the metal cools, heat it again as you are now going to have to bend the fishtail part.

14. With the metal still glowing hot, place the fishtail over the horn of the anvil closest to its tip.

15. Use the flat face of the hammer to hammer the fish tale around the part of the horn. You are creating a small hook, not a complete one, so it should not go all the way around. It should resemble a semi-circle.

16. Cool that part of the metal down to keep the hook shape.

17. Now you are going to want to create the handle.

18. Staying on the side of the small hook you have just created, you will have to heat the metal about 3 inches down from the small hook you have just created.

19.

20. You are going to essentially be creating an S-shape with a small top bend and a larger belly with the hook you just created. Sort of like the rough drawing above.

21. With the small hook facing upwards and towards you, place the heated part of the metal against the horn of the anvil.

22. Using the flat face of the hammer, hammer just below the small hook on the metal to make it start to bend around the horn or the anvil.

23. You do not want to make it completely round, more of an oblong-type shape. As it starts to bend around, pull it off the horn of the anvil.

24. Quickly as not to lose any of the heat, place the metal back on the table of the anvil. Balance the edge just below the glowing hot curve on the side of the anvils table. The inside of the glowing hot curve should be facing towards you.

25. Using the flat head side of the hammer, holding the metal stable as you hammer the top part that needs to fold back on itself and towards you down until it is almost flat against the straight part of the metal. In other words, you are closing up the handle portion.

26. Once it has been closed up, turn it onto either side to hammer it flat and ensure it is lined up correctly and straight.

27. Cool the handle off by dipping it into the water.

28. This part is going to take some time to do depending on how many twists you are going to want to put in the metal.

29. Heat the metal in the center of the bar.

30. When it is glowing hot, place it in the clamp.

31. Using pliers to grip the metal just about where you want to place the twist, turn it until you see a pattern.

32. Move the pliers up a bit and give it another twist; keep going until you have enough twists.

33. You may need to heat small sections of the metal at a time if you are doing a lot of twists. This is to let one piece of the twist cool and harden to get the next twist without messing up the previous one.

34. For doing twists like this, it is nice to have a cutting torch or plumbers torch, as you can heat small sections of the metal at a time with it locked in the vice. Until you get the hang of doing twists, this is a nifty little trick.

35. When you have enough twists, release the metal from the vice grip and cool it down.

36. Try not to go overboard or get too fancy with your design on your first time as things could go wrong and you may have to end up starting all over again.

37. Give it a good rub down with the hard brush to polish it up a bit and get rid of any residue leftover from heating and hammering the steel.

38. If you want to you can go ahead and smooth (planish) the stick to get a nice well-rounded and finished piece.

CHAPTER 3: PROJECT 2 – MAKING A DECORATIVE LEAF

This is a really simple and easy to make leaf keychain that teaches you how to create something a little more decorative. At the end of it, you will have a nice leaf you can use to put your car keys on or give someone as an authentic handcrafted gift.

What you will need:

- **A heat source** — your choice of a forge and either solid or gas fuel. It could be a plumber torch that use to heat metal pipes or even a cutters torch.
- **An anvil** — make sure your anvil has a flat table and horn. It should be the right height that is comfortable for you to work on. It must also be completely stable and steady that it does not move when you hammer on top of it or move when you press the metal hard against it to pound on.
- **Water** — a tin can with cold water will do nicely. Do not use plastic as you will be putting extremely hot metal into it.
- **Hammer** — choose a hammer that is not too heavy, around 1.5 to 2.5 lbs. The cross peen hammer is a good fit for this project or you could use the rounding hammers.

- **Tongs** — flat-faced tongs to hold and grip the metal with.
- **Vice Grip** — this is to hold the metal steady.
- **Metal** — ⅜-inch square stock.
- **Hard brush** — to dust the residue off the metal when you are done heating and pound it.
- **Chisel** – fine-edged chisel that is strong enough to withstand a hit from the hammer and able to withstand the heat from the metal.
- **Cutting Hardie** — this is an accessory that fits into the Hardie hole. It is a flat piece of metal that is used to cut off heated metal.
- **Round nose pliers** — to make a loop in the heated metal.

Method

1. Ready your forge and make sure it is burning nice and hot.
2. Have all your tools handy and ready to use, so you do not have to go searching for them.
3. Heat the top of the metal rod until the metal is glowing hot.
4. Place it with the tip flat on the tabletop of the anvil.
5. Use the flat face of the hammer to pound the tip of the metal into a point.
6. To do this you hit, then turn the metal to the next side, pound again and again as you turn the metal from side to side.

7. It will start to taper to a point that looks like a chiseled pencil point.

8. You will know when it is done at the end.

9. Now place the metal at the far edge of the anvil with the pointed part hanging about ½ inch off the anvil.

10. You are going to make a step shape on one side of the neck of the heated metal. You are going to want to turn it and make a dip in the heated metal on the other side. You are trying to draw the metal out and give it a nice thin neck.

11. The metal will look a bit like an arrow with a tapered head and a thin neck.

12. Once the neck has been done you are going to flatten the head into a leaf shape.

13. Heat the tip until the metal is glowing hot.

14. Place the tapered end on the body of the anvil.

15. Still using the flat side of the hammer, you are going to pound the pointed part flat.

16. Be careful not to hit the tip of the taper. Rather hit the thicker, bulbous part of where the metal tapers.

17. Hit the metal evenly on the bulb part until it starts to flatten and spread.

18. You should see it taking shape like a leaf.

19. Keep going until you see the body of the leaf has nicely formed.

20. Make sure the leaf part is still hot. You will have to be careful with the leaf part of the metal as it has now become a lot thinner, so it will heat up a lot quicker, and you do not want to melt it.

21. Take the peen side of the hammer and you are going to hit the left texture into metal using the hammer.

22. Hold the heated metal steady with the leaf shape on the anvil. With the peen side of the hammer, hit the leaf up one side. You should see a nice texture that looks like leaf veins start to take shape.

23. Do the same for the other side. Try to use just the edge of the peen to hit the leaf so you can get it to look like leaf veins. You will need to pound it on both the left and right sides of the leaf.

24. You need to do this on both the back and front of the left so the pattern appears on the front and back.

25. Leave the tip on the leaf a little thicker than the rest of the leaf.

26. Now to do the centerline of the leaf. This will be done with the chisel.

27. Give the leaf a bit of heat. Not too much as you do not want to melt all the hard work you have done on the pattern of the leaf.

28. Place the head of the leaf back on the body of the anvil.

29. Take the chisel and you are going to chisel it up the center of the leaf. You place the chisel on the leaf and then hit it with the hammer to pierce the metal. Try to chisel it in a slight curve.

30. Repeat the centerline on the back of the leaf as well.

31. Your leaf is done.

32. Now for the part where you make it into a key-chain.

33. As it is now, the body is far too long, so you are going to need to cut it off.

34. For this you are going to use the sheering method.

35. If you have a cutting Hardie, you are going to want to mount it in the Hardie hole.

36. Don't worry if you do not have a cutting Hardie, you can use the edge of the anvil just as easily.

37. Heat the metal about 2-½ inches above the leaf shape you have just created.

38. If you are using the Hardie attachment, place the heated part of the metal over the attachment with the leaf part extended.

39. Using the flat face of the hammer, you are going to hit the metal part that is resting on the cutting Hardie. You must make sure the metal part resting on the cutting Hardie is the part where you want to sever the metal.

40. Hit the metal by turning it after every hit.

41. You will see the metal start to thin in the neck until it is ready to break off.

42. If you do not have the cutting Hardie attachment, use the far end of the anvil table to get the same results. You only need to strike the metal right near the edge of the anvil in order to create the thin neck in the heated metal that will finally share it.

43. You may even need to reheat the metal if it cools too much while you are trying to wear it down enough to have it cut off.

44. Once the long side of the rod had been broken off the next part is to bend the stem of the leaf into a round loop for the key chain.

45. To do this, you need to use the flat-faced tongs to hold the leaf so you can heat the stem.

46. The first thing is to pound the stem into a nice round stem with a chiseled end.

47. To do this pound the heated metal with the flat end of the hammer, turning over and hitting it once or twice on every turn.

48. As you round it off, you will also be drawing the metal out and extending it.

49. Give the stem a bit more heat, then take a pair of round-nose pliers. You are going to twist the stem right around into a loop for the end where the key chain is going to be.

50. Cool it down.

51. Give it a good scrub with the brush to buff it up and the keychain should be ready.

CHAPTER 4: PROJECT 3 – MAKING A LETTER OPENER

This project is to make a simple letter opener using some of the more basic tools of the blacksmith trade.

What you will need:

- **A heat source** — a gas or coal forge of your choice or heat source that you have access to.
- **An anvil** — this does not have to be the top-of-the-line anvil, just one that has all the sturdy properties of an anvil and is at the right height for you to comfortably work with.
- **Water** — a tin can with cold water. Do not use a plastic container.
- **Hammer** — choose a hammer that is not too heavy; a cross peen hammer or a rounding hammer is fine for this project.
- **Tongs** — flat-faced tongs for a solid grip.
- **Metal** — 1-½-inch round stock about 12 inches long.
- **Hard brush** — to dust the residue off the metal.
- **Bending Hardie** — this is an accessory that fits into the Hardie hold to bend the metal.
- **Round nose pliers** — to make a loop in the heated metal.

Method

1. Ready your forge and make sure it is burning hot enough.
2. Get all your tools ready for use.
3. Heat the top of the metal rod until the metal is glowing hot.
4. The first thing we are going to do is upset the metal to make the end a lot thicker and condense the metal rod a bit.
5. Place the heated end of the metal onto the anvil with the metal bar standing upright.
6. You can either grip it with a tong or put it into a vice grip to keep it very steady. The cold end, which should be facing you, with the flat face of the cross peen hammer.
7. Keep hitting until the metal starts to get a bit fatter at the heated end.
8. As you want to localize the upsetting to around 2-½ to 3 inches of the tip, the rest of the bar is going to have to be cooled down.
9. Hang the metal bar just above the metal bucket or a can of cold water. Use a cup or your hand to sprinkle cold water over the parts of the bar you do not want to be affected by the upsetting.
10. As you hammer down the metal, stop and round it off by hitting it on the sides.

11. Once it has grown a bit thicker in size, you are going to want to cool it off in the bucket of cold water.

12. This is going to be the handle side of the letter opener.

13. Next, heat the other end of the metal until it is glowing hot.

14. Now it needs to be tapered into a point using the flat side of the hammer once again.

15. You want to draw out the metal and taper as you have done with the other two projects.

16. You do this by putting the side heated side onto the table of the anvil and then use the flat face of the hammer to knock it out into a point.

17. Once you have a point on it, you are going to flatten it into a nice sharp flat blade for your letter opener.

18. You may need to reheat the metal then, still using the flat face of the hammer, hit the point flat against the table of the anvil. You can give it a nice tapering look to resemble the shape of a knife by flattening the tip of the point first then moving to the bulb part of the taper.

19. Be sure to even out both sides of the blade.

20. The next step is to bevel the edge of the letter opener blade.

21. To do this, you will line the blade end up with the edge of the anvil.

22. To apply the bevel to the edges, you will need to hit the metal at the very edge of it. The strike will hit the edge of the heated metal and bounce off the edge of the anvil in an angled strike.

23. Do this along the length of the blade on both sides of the blade head (the left and right side)
24. Once the blade has been smoothed out and beveled, it is time to cool it off in the cold water.
25. Give it a good brush off with the hard brush.
26. Now back to shape the handle of the letter opener.
27. Place the Hardie curving tool securely in the Hardie hole.
28. Heat the top of the letter opener (the end that you upset and thickened at the beginning of the project) until the metal is glowing hot.
29. Place the heated part in between the two poles of the bending accessory in the Hardie hole.
30. Grip the longer end of the steel with a clamp. The clamp will help you switch the metal around the pillar of the Hardie hole tool.
31. Using the flat face of the hammer, start to hammer the metal and bend it around the pillar until it forms a nice umbrella handle hook.
32. You may have to reheat the metal again at this point.
33. When it is glowing hot, place the section with the umbrella hook on the flat tabletop of the anvil.
34. The hook should be pointing towards you.
35. Knock it down to join it to the metal to close the loop using the flat face of the hammer.
36. Cool off the head of the letter opener.
37. Heat the body of the letter open until it is glowing hot.
38. Place the letter opener handle in the jaws of a vice grip.

39. Using pliers, grip the metal in the center and make a twist.
40. Move the pliers up a section and make another twist.
41. Repeat this motion until you have two to four nice metal twists.
42. Cool the letter opener down.
43. Once it has cooled off, give it a nice brushing off with the hard-bristled brush.
44. You can apply a nice hot wax to it if you want to give it a nice buff shine. You can get special wax at a hardware store. Be sure to follow the instructions on the wax on how to apply it.

CONCLUSION

Blacksmithing is a true art form and is a skill that you get better at the more you practice. When you are just starting, do not worry about getting the biggest or the best equipment – get the basics. If the basics are out of your budget, you can improvise. As long as you have a decent forging hammer, anvil, and a heat source hot enough to heat up metal to a point it can be manipulated, you are well on your way.

As you get into the trade, you can start to collect tools to build up your sets. Some blacksmiths even make their own tools. There is nothing like seeing a box of tools made by your own hands adorning your tool wall.

It is also a nice hobby that can make you some extra cash on the side. Handcrafted metalwork tends to be a hit at various craft shows and markets. Another great seller for metal forgers is furniture, gates, and even handmade cutlery, pots, and pans. There is so much mass-produced stuff on the market that people are always on the lookout for something that's different and authentic.

In this day and age, you do not even have to go to the market to sell your metalwork; you can do so online. With social media and websites being what they are today, all you need is a clever marketing strategy and you could be taking orders for your metal creations in no time.

Remember to practice good housekeeping by always keeping your tools, chimney, and forge clean. This not only prolongs the life of your tools, but it also cuts down on the cost of having to replace them or get them fixed.

It is a very enjoyable and rewarding trade to be in. There is nothing like the feeling of being able to forge metal into something you have imagined. Keep practicing and don't let little speed bumps, hiccups, getting it wrong, etc., get in your way. Even the pros can have bad designs and mess up, so keep going, and if at first, you don't succeed, try until you do. It is metal, and you can reuse it a few times over!

REFERENCES

Blaszczak-Boxe, A. (2017, August 23). Facts About Iron. Retrieved from https://www.livescience.com/29263-iron.html

History.com (n.d.). Iron Age. Retrieved from https://www.history.com/topics/pre-history/iron-age

Jefferson Lab. (n.d.). The Element Iron. Retrieved from https://education.jlab.org/itselemental/ele026.html

Joey99. (n.d.). Start Blacksmithing. Retrieved from https://www.instructables.com/id/Start-Blacksmithing/

Los Alamos National Laboratory. (n.d.). Periodic Table of Elements: LANL. Retrieved from https://periodic.lanl.gov/26.shtml

Noble Forge. (n.d.). History of Blacksmithing. Retrieved from http://www.nobleforge.com/history-of-blacksmithing/

Royal Society of Chemistry. (n.d.). Iron. Retrieved from https://www.rsc.org/periodic-table/element/26/iron

ScienceDirect. (2013). 5,000 years old Egyptian iron beads made from hammered meteoritic iron. Retrieved from https://www.sciencedirect.com/science/article/pii/S0305440313002057

Storm Castle.com. (n.d.). Blacksmithing lesson 5: Hammer Strikes [Video File]. Retrieved from https://www.youtube.com/watch?v=0GQl-oqFTnc&feature=youtu.be

The Consummate Dabbler. (2014, April 23). Essentials of Blacksmithing [Video File]. Retrieved from https://www.youtube.com/watch?v=ZToka1-8oQA&list=PLlrjOezwxajaynwjWUH38heo-hjPS7ziMp&index=13

Printed in the USA
CPSIA information can be obtained
at www.ICGtesting.com
LVHW012022020224
770774LV00003B/250